SHOW ME HOW
I Can Paint

Arty activities for kids
shown step by step

PETRA BOASE

ARMADILLO

This edition is published by Armadillo,
an imprint of Anness Publishing Ltd

www.armadillobooks.co.uk; www.annesspublishing.com;
Twitter: @Anness_Books

If you like the images in this book and would like to investigate using
them for publishing, promotions or advertising, please visit our
website www.practicalpictures.com for more information.

Publisher: Joanna Lorenz
Project Editors: Clare Nicholson and Richard McGinlay
Photographer: John Freeman
Designer: Edward Kinsey
Production Controller: Stephanie Moe

ACKNOWLEDGEMENTS
The publishers would like to thank the following children for
appearing in this book, and of course their parents: Alice, Aron,
Jessica, Joshua, Kirsty, Nicholas, Sasha, Tania and Venetia.

PUBLISHER'S NOTE
The level of adult supervision will depend on the ability and age of the
children following the projects. However, we advise that adult
supervision is always preferable, and vital if the project calls for the use
of sharp knives or other utensils. Always keep potentially dangerous
tools and products well out of the reach of young children.
Although the advice and information in this book are believed to be
accurate and true at the time of going to press, neither the authors nor
the publisher can accept any legal responsibility or liability for any
errors or omissions that may have been made nor for any inaccuracies
nor for any loss, harm or injury that comes about from following
instructions or advice in this book.

Manufacturer: Anness Publishing Ltd, 108 Great Russell Street,
London WC1B 3NA, England
For Product Tracking go to: www.annesspublishing.com/tracking
Batch: 7212-23008-1127

Contents

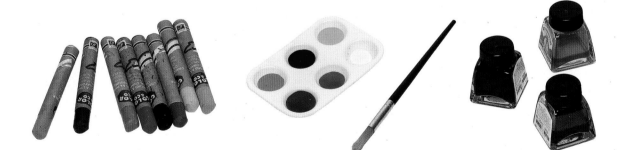

Introduction

Painting is fun, but painting does not necessarily mean standing at an easel copying what you see in front of you – although you can do that, too, if you want. The projects in this book show you how to have lots of fun with different sorts of paints on lots of different surfaces.

None of the projects in this book is difficult, although there are a few things you should do before you begin.

1 Carefully read through the list of materials you will need.

2 Read through the instructions and look at the photographs so that you have a clear idea of what you will be doing.

3 Assemble everything you need before you start on a project.

4 Some of the projects are messy and some aren't, but it is always a good idea to cover your work surface with newspaper, scrap paper or a piece of material. If you are working on a wipe-clean surface and doing one of the less messy projects, this is not essential, but it is a good idea to get into the habit.

5 Wear an old shirt or a painting overall and, when you have finished, always clear away everything you have used.

You may not want a grown-up around while you are being creative, but there are some things that you will need help with. Some of the projects call for sharp scissors and you may prefer a grown-up to do the cutting for you. Some types of cardboard are easier to cut with a craft knife. These knives are very sharp and are quite tricky to use, so always get a grown-up to do any cutting with a craft knife. Always ask a grown-up to mix and thin oil paints for you as well. You can mix other kinds of paint such as watercolour and poster paint yourself.

Wear an old shirt or painting overall.

Before you begin, make sure you have everything you will need.

Mixing paints

You don't need a lot of different shades of paint to do the projects. It is easy to mix lots of paints, as long as you have the three primary shades: red, blue and yellow.

Red + Blue = Purple
Red + Yellow = Orange
Blue + Yellow = Green

You can make different sorts of browns by mixing purple and orange, orange and green and purple and green.

If you start off with red, yellow and blue and, perhaps, white (with which you can make paler versions of the other shades), you can easily add more shades of paint as your pocket money allows. You will also need black paint for some of the projects, so check before you begin.

Be careful when you use scissors.

Templates

Some of the projects in this book have pattern templates for you to trace. You will find these on the following pages.

1 Place a sheet of tracing paper over the template pattern in the book. Hold the paper in position with your spare hand. Carefully trace the pattern using a soft pencil.

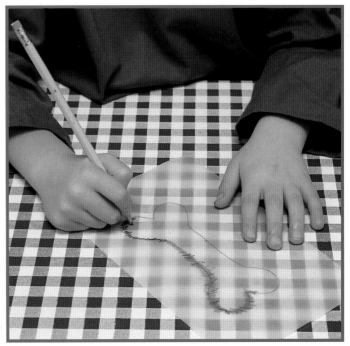

2 To transfer your pattern on to cardboard or paper, turn the tracing paper over and scribble over the outline with your pencil.

3 Turn the sheet of tracing paper over again and place it on your sheet of cardboard. Draw around the outline of the pattern firmly. It will transfer on to the paper or cardboard.

4 Remove the tracing paper and make sure that all the pattern has been transferred. Cut out the template, and then draw around it as shown in the project pictures.

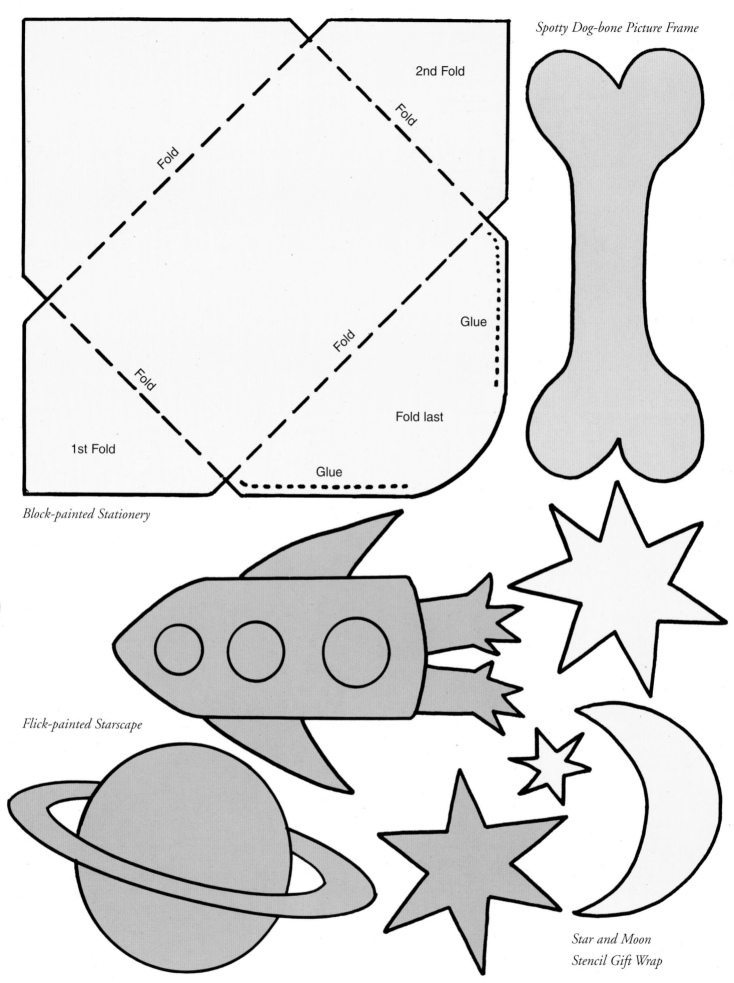

Spotty Dog-bone Picture Frame

2nd Fold

Fold

Fold

Fold

Glue

Fold

Fold last

1st Fold

Glue

Block-painted Stationery

Flick-painted Starscape

*Star and Moon
Stencil Gift Wrap*

Christmas Crackers

Flowery Glass

Equipment

These are the general pieces of equipment that you will need throughout the book. Other items are listed individually for the relevant project.

Paint palette If you don't have a paint palette, you can use an old plate or saucer. Remember to wash whatever you use thoroughly at the end of a project and don't use a plate to eat from once it has been used for paint.

Plastic cups These make ideal containers for mixing paints in, but you can't drink from them afterwards. Alternatives are clean food or coffee jars.

Adhesive tape This is available in a variety of widths and shades and is useful for sticking small things together.

Painting beakers Painting beakers with lids allow you to store runny paint from session to session.

Cloth It is always a good idea to have a cloth with you when you are working on a project, just in case you have an accident and you need to clean it up quickly.

Pencils Soft pencils are best for tracing out templates and for drawing out designs before painting.

Eraser If you make a mistake when drawing with a pencil, you can simply rub it out.

Pencil sharpener Use this to keep your pencil sharp – which makes it easier to draw clean lines.

Paintbrushes These are available in many different shapes and sizes. If you are painting large areas, use bigger brushes and, if you are painting fine lines, use thinner brushes. In order to make them last, you must look after them, washing them out in cold water after using them with water-based paints or in turpentine or white spirit if you have used them with oil-based paints.

Ruler A ruler is useful for measuring and for drawing straight lines.

Scissors Scissors are used for cutting out paper. Always have a grown-up close by when you are using scissors.

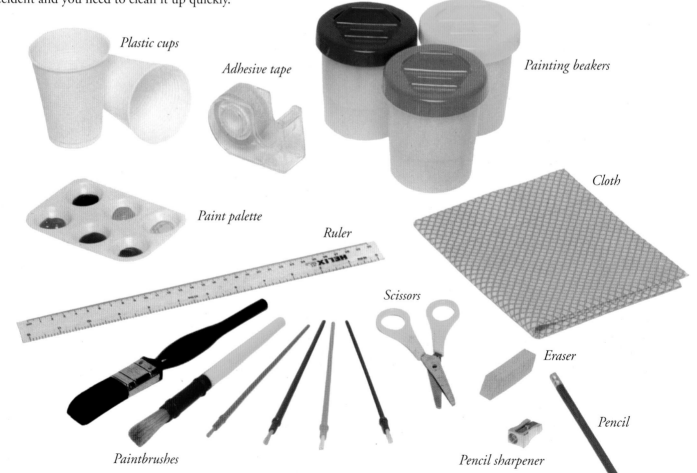

Plastic cups

Adhesive tape

Painting beakers

Cloth

Paint palette

Ruler

Scissors

Eraser

Paintbrushes

Pencil sharpener

Pencil

Materials

Each type of paint is different and takes a different amount of time to dry. Always read the instructions on the pot or tube before you start.

Acrylic paint This is rubber-based, flat and opaque so that it covers large areas easily but does not have the shine of oil paint or the texture of water-based paint.

Poster paint This is water-based and is available either as a powder to be mixed with water, or ready-mixed.

Fabric paint Fabric paint is necessary for painting or printing on textiles. Each type is different so read the instructions carefully and clean your brushes accordingly.

Inks These are available in a wide variety of shades. If you can't find any, or can't get the shade you want, you can use food dyes instead. Always make sure they are washable.

Oil paints These are very greasy and must be handled with care. Ask a grown-up to mix white spirit or turpentine with oil paints to thin them. Ask an adult to clean your brushes with white spirit or turpentine.

Wax crayons These are used in wax-resist paintings. If you don't have any crayons, you can use candles instead.

White glue Also known as PVA glue, this is an all-purpose adhesive for paper and cardboard. Keep it away from your mouth and follow the instructions on the container. Use a brush or a glue spreader to put it on.

Cardboard This comes in many different thicknesses. If you are making a template from cardboard, you will need thin cardboard. For this, you could use a cereal packet. If you need thick cardboard, try using a cardboard box.

Tracing paper Tracing paper is a clear paper necessary for the projects that involve tracing over templates. Use greaseproof paper as an alternative.

Paper This is available in a variety of shades and weights. Cartridge or construction paper is a good-quality kind of heavy paper for painting and drawing on. For some of the projects, lining paper (which is available from do-it-yourself stores) will give good results and is much cheaper. Some of the projects call for non-white paper, which you can get from stationers and craft stores.

Poster paints

Fabric paints

White glue

Wax crayons

Acrylic paints

Oil paints

Inks

Star and Moon Stencil Gift Wrap

If you have always wanted to make your own special gift wrap and matching greetings cards, now is your chance.

The moon and star shapes that Kirsty is making are simple. She is only using gold paint, but you can use lots of different shades. If you want to stencil with lots of shades, use a different sponge for each paint and let each one dry thoroughly before you add the next.

Stencil technique

Stencils are great fun and easy to use. For the best results, the paint needs to be thick, so don't mix any water with it. Do not use too much paint on the sponge, and apply it with a light dabbing movement. You can always go over it again to add more depth.

YOU WILL NEED THESE MATERIALS AND TOOLS

Tracing paper

Soft pencil

Thin cardboard

Scissors

Paper in the shade of your choice

Reusable putty adhesive

Sponge

Gold paint

Palette or saucer

Ribbon

Hole punch

1 Using a soft pencil, trace the star and moon templates from the front of the book on to cardboard.

2 Use the scissors to make a hole in the middle of the design, and then cut towards the shape. You should have three different stencils.

3 Place the stencils on the paper. Secure them with reusable putty adhesive. Dab the sponge in the gold paint and sponge over the stencils.

4 Let the paint dry, then move the stencils to another space on the paper and repeat. Continue until you have covered the whole sheet with gold moons and stars.

5 When the paint is completely dry, use the sheet of paper to wrap up a present. To make the gift extremely luxurious, add a gold ribbon and tie a bow.

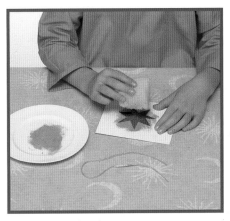

6 Cut out a small piece of paper and stencil it in the same way to make a gift tag for the present. Using a hole punch, make a hole in the corner and slip a piece of gold ribbon through.

7 Here a moon is being painted on to a card for a different design.

A unique set of gift wrap for a very special present.

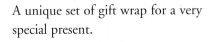

Christmas Crackers

Your family and friends will be delighted when you present them with these pretty crackers at the Christmas meal or at a party. You must plan this project in advance as you need a cardboard tube for each cracker.

Jessica is using traditional Christmas shapes and shades in her design, but you could choose your own instead.

Presents galore

If you are feeling generous you could also put a little gift inside each cracker, and perhaps write a joke to go inside as well. This should be done in step 7, when you have closed only one end of the cracker.

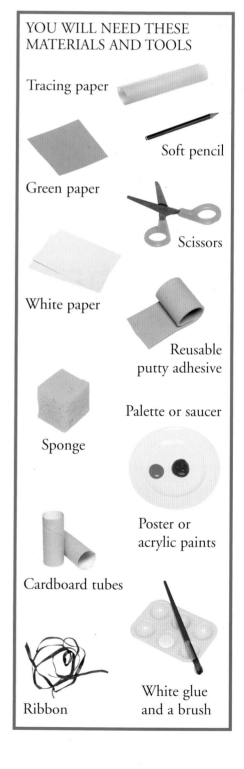

YOU WILL NEED THESE MATERIALS AND TOOLS

Tracing paper

Soft pencil

Green paper

Scissors

White paper

Reusable putty adhesive

Palette or saucer

Sponge

Poster or acrylic paints

Cardboard tubes

Ribbon

White glue and a brush

1 Trace the holly leaf and Christmas tree templates from the front of the book on to green paper. Cut them out.

2 Arrange the shapes over the white paper, sticking them down with a piece of reusable putty adhesive. Your pattern can be regular or random.

3 Dab the sponge into one of the paints. Wipe off any excess on the side of the palette. Sponge over all the shapes on the paper.

4 Rinse the sponge under running water, squeezing it as dry as you can. Dab it in the second shade of paint and sponge over the shapes again.

5 When the sheet of paper is completely dry, gently peel the templates away to reveal an attractive Christmas design. Place it face down on your work surface.

6 Brush glue all over the cardboard tube. Place it halfway along one edge of the sheet of paper. Carefully roll the paper around the tube. Glue the edge down.

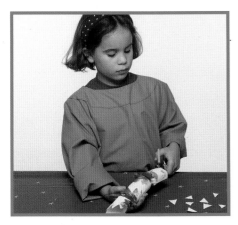

7 Feel where the ends of the tube are and pinch in the paper there. Finally, cut triangles from the ends of the paper and add ribbons.

The ideal table decoration for a Christmas party.

Painted Stones Caterpillar

Once you have painted these pebbles with pictures or numbers, you will have hours of fun with them. Joshua is being clever with his pebbles by painting a caterpillar on one side and numbers and mathematical signs on the other, so that he can learn his sums and see how brainy he is.

If you are unable to get to the beach to collect pebbles, make some from self-hardening clay, which can be bought in craft and hobby stores.

Painting tips

You will find it easier to paint half of all the stones, and then go back and finish them off. In this way, you won't be trying to hold an area of stone that is already wet.

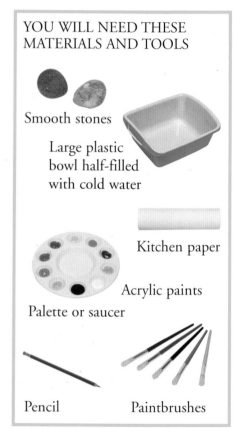

YOU WILL NEED THESE
MATERIALS AND TOOLS

Smooth stones

Large plastic
bowl half-filled
with cold water

Kitchen paper

Acrylic paints

Palette or saucer

Pencil   Paintbrushes

1 Wash the stones in the plastic bowl and dry them well with kitchen paper. Use as many stones as you like.

2 Paint the stones. Try to make each one a different shade. Leave them on your work surface until they are completely dry.

3 Arrange the stones in a long line with the biggest at one end and the smallest at the other. Draw a caterpillar design on them.

4 Paint the caterpillar's body using different shades. Use black, brown or another dark paint for its feet.

5 Decorate each part of its body with different spots. You can vary the size of the spots, too.

6 Either use a new set of painted stones, or wait until the caterpillar is dry and turn the stones over. Paint in some figures and mathematical symbols.

7 Impress your family and friends by showing them how clever you are.

None of your papers will blow away when the stone caterpillar is standing on top of them!

Butterfly Blottography Box

Blottography prints are easy to do and the results are always an exciting surprise. This technique is over 100 years old. Alice is using her prints to brighten up a storage box, but you could also stick a blottography shape to a tray and varnish over it – ask a grown-up to help with this.

Blottography technique
Be sure to use a large piece of paper for your prints so that paint doesn't ooze out over everything and make a mess.

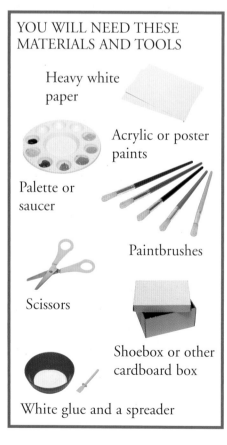

YOU WILL NEED THESE MATERIALS AND TOOLS

Heavy white paper

Acrylic or poster paints

Palette or saucer

Paintbrushes

Scissors

Shoebox or other cardboard box

White glue and a spreader

1 Make sure that your sheet of paper is longer than it is wide. Fold it in half lengthways.

2 Open up the paper and dab generous spots of paint on one side only. Use as many different paints as you like, but don't get them *too* runny.

3 Fold the paper in half once again, bringing the dry side over on to the wet side. Carefully smooth it down with your hand.

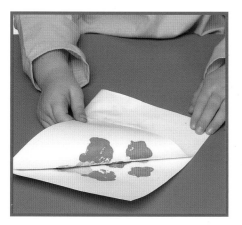

4 Open up the paper and admire the bright, symmetrical pattern you have created on both sides of the paper. Leave it to dry thoroughly.

5 Make some more patterns of different sizes and using different paint combinations in the same way. Try using all pale paints or all dark. Cut them out when they are dry.

6 Paint the cardboard box inside and out. If you are using a shoebox, or any other box that was not white to start with, you will find it easier to cover the existing shade if you use acrylic paint. Poster paint is fine if your box is white to start with.

An attractive way of storing all your odds and ends.

7 When the box is completely dry, glue your patterns on to it.

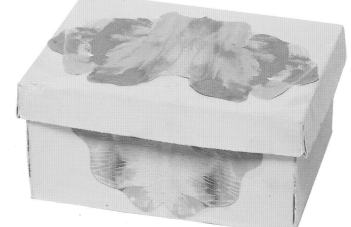

Vegetable-print T-shirt

Sasha is using different shades and all sorts of vegetables on a white T-shirt. If you don't want to make an all-over design, you could print just in the middle of the shirt. For a more intricate design, use smaller vegetables such as tiny onions cut in half, or a baby carrot. Use different sizes of mushroom, too.

Design rules

If you are not sure about a design, print it on paper first to get a good idea of how it will look when it is on the T-shirt. Once it is on the T-shirt it will be difficult to remove or change.

YOU WILL NEED THESE MATERIALS AND TOOLS

Selection of vegetables

Chopping board

Kitchen knife

Plain T-shirt, preferably white

Newspaper

Fabric paints

Paintbrushes

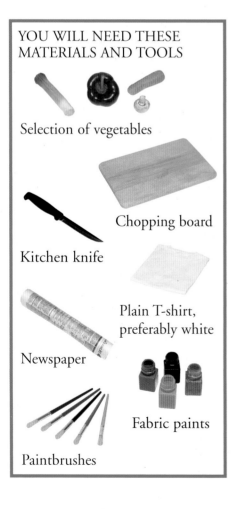

1 Choose vegetables that will make interesting prints of different sizes, such as a stick of celery (semicircle), carrot (circle), pepper (crinkly circle), mushroom and leek.

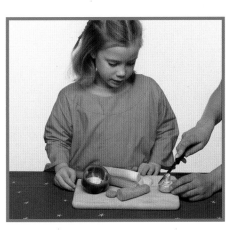

2 Ask a grown-up to cut up the vegetables for you. Make sure that they cut round the pepper – you don't want a strip – and leave the stalk on the mushroom slice.

3 Lay the T-shirt flat and front side up on your work surface. Put some newspapers inside so that your design does not go through to the back of the T-shirt.

4 Paint the edge of the pepper with fabric paint. Make sure that the edge is covered with paint but don't get it too wet or it might smudge.

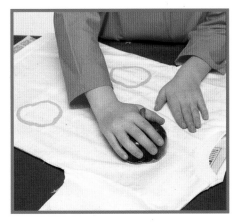

5 Print the pepper on to the T-shirt. Try to hold it still while it is in contact with the shirt so that the edges don't blur. You may need to repaint it between prints.

6 Paint the end of the carrot with fabric paint and use it to print in the middle of and all around the pepper prints. Try not to print over another print as the paints may run together. Use all the other vegetables in the same way.

7 Choose different paints for each vegetable, building up an interesting design. Leave to dry.

Everyone will want to know where you got your designer T-shirt!

Disco Dazzler T-shirt

Wear this wild T-shirt to be the focus of attention. The patterns will positively glow in the dark under ultraviolet light. This is because they have been painted using fluorescent fabric paint.

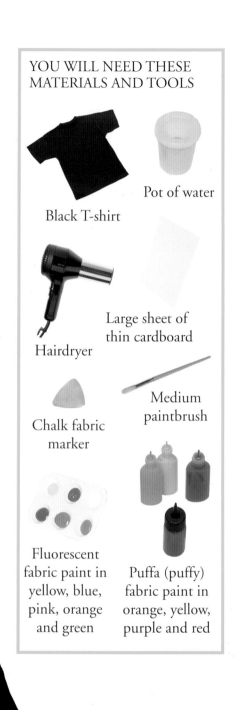

YOU WILL NEED THESE MATERIALS AND TOOLS

Black T-shirt

Pot of water

Hairdryer

Large sheet of thin cardboard

Chalk fabric marker

Medium paintbrush

Fluorescent fabric paint in yellow, blue, pink, orange and green

Puffa (puffy) fabric paint in orange, yellow, purple and red

1 Insert pieces of cardboard inside the body and sleeves of the T-shirt. Use the chalk fabric marker to draw the outlines of triangles, spirals and zigzag patterns all over the front and the sleeves. Draw a zigzag pattern along the bottom edge of the T-shirt.

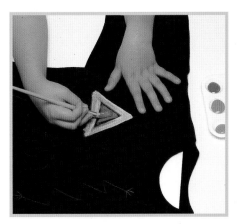

2 Use fluorescent yellow, blue, pink, orange and green fabric paint to fill in the outlines. To make other shades, simply mix different shades together on a palette. Allow the fabric paint to dry before painting patterns on to areas already painted.

3 Decorate the T-shirt with dots and squiggles of orange, yellow, purple and red puffa fabric paint. You can make your patterns as wild as you like. To make the puffa fabric paint puff up, dry it with a hairdryer. Set the hairdryer to its coolest setting.

4 Go over the zigzag at the bottom of the T-shirt with orange puffa fabric paint. Use other puffa fabric paints to add circles and dots. Once again, use the hairdryer set to its coolest temperature to dry the puffa fabric paint. Allow your T-shirt to dry thoroughly before hitting the disco and dazzling all your friends!

If you want to continue the zigzag pattern on the back of the T-shirt, wait for the front to dry before turning the T-shirt over. Before starting to paint, check that the cardboard is still in place.

Party paints

Though this design looks great in fluorescent fabric paint, it can also be done using bright plain fabric paints. Even though these paints will not glow in the dark, your T-shirt will still be the envy of all at the disco. But if you like a bit of glitz and glitter, why not use glitter fabric paint or fabric glitter?

Fierce Leopard Face Paint

As well as wearing paint on your clothes, you can also wear it on you! Face painting is a great way to be transformed into an animal, especially an exotic jungle creature like this sleek, spotted leopard.

To make your face look lean, mean and hungry, the outline around the face is a special shape.

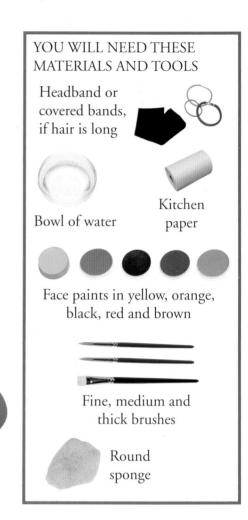

YOU WILL NEED THESE MATERIALS AND TOOLS

Headband or covered bands, if hair is long

Bowl of water

Kitchen paper

Face paints in yellow, orange, black, red and brown

Fine, medium and thick brushes

Round sponge

Handy hint

If you use face paint on your hands, do not forget to keep your hands away from water. Even small splashes of water will wash away face paint.

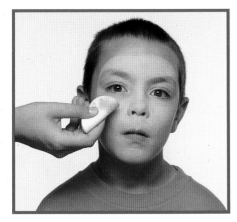

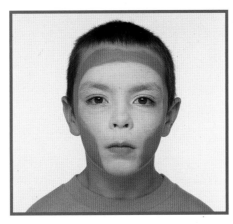

1 Tie the hair back, if necessary. Paint a yellow circle around the face with a medium brush. Fill in the circle with yellow face paint applied with a round sponge. Try to apply the face paint smoothly and evenly.

2 Use the thick brush to paint an outline around the face in orange face paint. Shape the outline, as shown. Neaten the edges with the fine or medium brush. Allow the base paint to dry thoroughly before continuing.

3 Close your eyes while black lines are painted on your eyelids. A fine brush will be needed for this. Paint the nose and the upper lip with black face paint. Paint the line that runs from the upper lip to the nose.

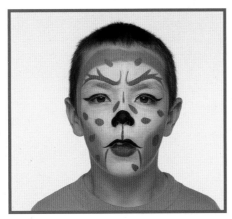

4 Even leopards can raise a smile so that their lower lip can be painted bright red. A fine brush will be needed to paint the lips.

5 Use the fine brush to paint the sweeping eyebrows, spots and lines on the face brown. Try to do this as neatly as possible.

6 Paint tiny brown dots below the nose with the fine brush. Paint lines from these dots to make the leopard's whiskers. Growl!

Look out, there's a leopard about!

To make yourself a really convincing leopard takes a little more than just face paint. You will have to prowl like a leopard – silently – and growl like a leopard. It also helps if you dress like this sleek lord of the jungle.

To make the ears, cut two oval shapes from thin orange cardboard. Fold along the bottom to form a flap. Draw a line in felt-tip pen on each ear, as shown. Apply special make-up glue to the base of the flaps and press them on to your forehead. Adding spots to an orange T-shirt – and even jogging pants or leggings – is easy. Simply cut yellow circles from thin cardboard and use double-sided adhesive tape to attach them to the front and back of the T-shirt.

You can either paint the paws using face paint or wear a pair of gloves or socks on your hands. You can decorate the gloves or socks with circles and strips of thin cardboard. Attach the cardboard with double-sided adhesive tape.

Spotty Dog-bone Picture Frame

Framing

When making a picture frame, make sure that the hole in the middle of your frame is cut to the right size. Measure your picture before you begin and then make the hole slightly smaller than this. If the hole is too big, the backing sheet will show through.

Frame a picture of your pet with one of these fun frames. Nicholas is using a pretty photograph of his dog. Alternatively, you could frame your paintings and put on an exhibition of your works of art.

YOU WILL NEED THESE MATERIALS AND TOOLS

Tracing paper

White paper

Soft pencil

Scissors

Craft knife

Thick cardboard

Ruler

Palette or saucer

Thin cardboard

Acrylic or poster paints

Paintbrush

White glue and a spreader

Cord

Adhesive tape

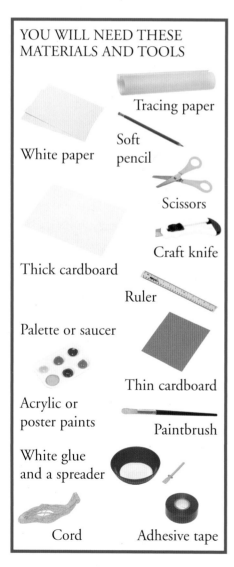

1 Using a soft pencil, trace the dog-bone template from the beginning of the book on to white paper. Make six copies.

2 Cut out the dog bone shapes using the scissors. Take care as you cut round the curves so that you get six even-looking bones.

3 Paint each bone. When the background has dried, paint on some spots. Don't choose very bright paints for either the bones or spots.

4 Ask a grown-up to cut the thin cardboard for the frame, and to cut out the middle. Cut a piece of thin cardboard slightly larger than the hole.

5 Paint the frame a plain shade that will look attractive with your bones and with the photograph you intend to display in the frame. Leave it to dry.

6 Glue the bones on to the frame. Push out any air bubbles with your fingers. If you have used too much glue, let it dry then peel it off.

7 Stick a loop of cord to the top of the back of the frame. Then attach the backing card with tape, leaving the top free to slip your photograph inside.

A special frame for a special photograph.

27

Marbled Pencils and Pencil Pot

The exciting thing about marbled papers is that each sheet is different and unique. Marbling is simple to do, but always ask a grown-up to mix the oil paint as you must not get turpentine near your eyes or mouth. You can buy ready-mixed marbling paints from craft or hobby stores.

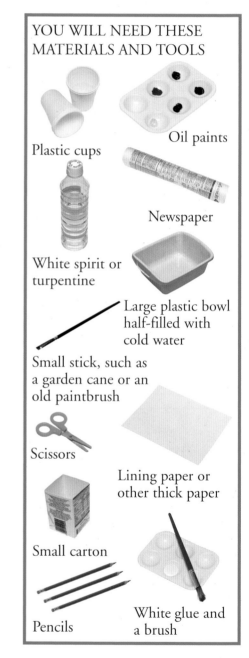

YOU WILL NEED THESE MATERIALS AND TOOLS

Plastic cups

Oil paints

White spirit or turpentine

Newspaper

Large plastic bowl half-filled with cold water

Small stick, such as a garden cane or an old paintbrush

Scissors

Lining paper or other thick paper

Small carton

Pencils

White glue and a brush

Marbling technique

The secret of good marbling is not to pour too much paint into the water at once. You can always add more after you have made one sheet of paper if you think it is too pale.

1 Squeeze a blob of about five different paints into separate plastic cups and ask a grown-up to add a small amount of turpentine. Mix well.

2 Cover your work surface with newspaper. Place the plastic bowl on the work surface. Gradually pour the oil paints into the water.

3 Mix the paints around to make interesting patterns. Make sure that you haven't got a big blob of one paint completely unmixed.

4 Cut a piece of paper about the same size as the plastic bowl and gently place it on the surface of the patterned water.

5 Remove the paper carefully and place it face up on a flat surface covered with newspaper. Try making different papers, experimenting with different shades and patterns.

6 When your papers are completely dry, use one to cover the carton. Cut it to shape, then glue it down. Leave some paper at the top to glue down inside the box.

7 Cover some pencils with your marbled paper so they match your pencil holder.

Cheer up homework time with your unique pencils and pot!

Bubble-printed Notebook

Food dye
If you can't find the right variety of inks, you could use food dyes instead. You may find that there are not as many different shades and most of them will be paler than some inks, but you will still get good results.

It is a good idea to do bubble printing as close to the kitchen sink as you can since you need lots of water and dishwashing detergent to make fluffy bubbles. Don't lift a full bowl of water yourself – ask a grown-up to do it.

The secret of bubble printing is not to pour in too many different shades at once. Remember you can always add more if you don't like the first sheet.

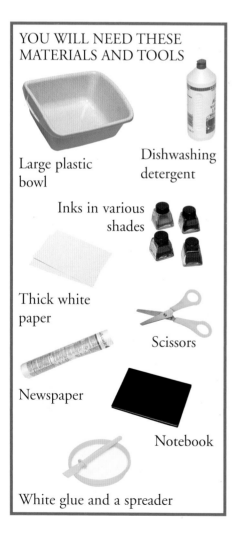

YOU WILL NEED THESE MATERIALS AND TOOLS

Large plastic bowl

Dishwashing detergent

Inks in various shades

Thick white paper

Scissors

Newspaper

Notebook

White glue and a spreader

1 Squeeze a generous amount of dishwashing detergent into the plastic bowl.

2 Add cold water and swish it around so that there are plenty of bubbles in the bowl.

3 Gradually dribble different shades of ink on to the surface of the bubbles in the bowl.

4 Cut a piece of thick paper to a size slightly smaller than the bowl. Gently lay the paper on the surface of the bubbles.

5 Carefully remove the paper from the bowl and place it face up on sheets of newspaper to dry.

6 If the paper dries crinkly, flatten it by placing it in between some heavy books and leaving it overnight.

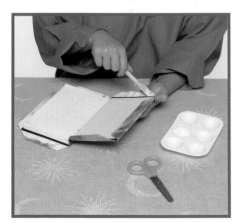

7 Cut the paper to fit the notebook, adding an extra 2.5cm/1in all around. Cut across the corners and cut a V at the top and bottom of the spine. Glue the overlap inside the cover.

Decorate your notebooks, diary and address book with your individual bubble-printed papers.

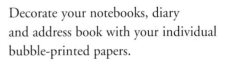

Wet-painted Table Mat and Coaster

These fun place mats are great for a party. Make one for each guest. Before you start, find a photograph of a rainbow. This will give you an idea of how different shades work together. The most exciting part of making these mats is watching the various inks run into each other, making new shades. Aron has made a coaster to match his mat.

Drying tip

Place your wet papers on to piles of newspaper to dry. It is a good idea to have your newspapers piled up and ready before you start.

YOU WILL NEED THESE MATERIALS AND TOOLS

Thick white paper

Scissors

Sponge

Paintbrush

Inks in various shades

Kitchen paper

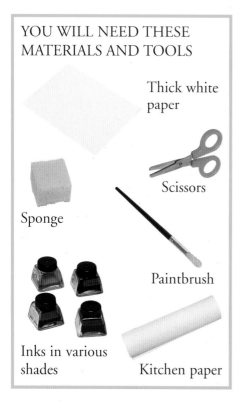

1 Cut the paper to about 20 x 30cm/ 8 x 12in. Wet the sponge, then squeeze it out and moisten the paper.

2 Load the paintbrush with ink, one shade at a time, and paint stripes down the paper.

3 Continue to paint stripes until you have covered the paper and the inks are all beginning to run together.

4 If there are any puddles of ink, take a piece of kitchen paper and blot them up. This will also add interest to the finished pattern.

5 When the paper is completely dry, make a series of small cuts along the two long edges to create a fringed effect to the mat.

6 Make a mat for a cup or glass in exactly the same way. A piece of thick paper 10 x 10cm/4 x 4in is ideal for this.

7 For other mats, change the pattern by painting circles and squares, leaving some areas of the paper unpainted if you like.

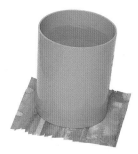

The ideal place settings for a party, or just to liven up every day.

Block-printed Stationery

You can make your own designer stationery using these block prints. Print different looking cards and envelopes and mix and match them when you send letters to friends. Experiment with different shapes and textures, such as bits of sponge and pasta shells.

Venetia's corrugated cardboard prints are very attractive. Repaint the print blocks between each print and, if you want to change shade, wipe the block clean with a cloth.

Gift cards

If you are using this stationery yourself, simply glue the envelope down with the letter inside. If you are making a set for a gift, add a small piece of double-sided tape to the flap of the envelope. Then the envelopes can be stuck down securely simply by peeling off the backing of the tape.

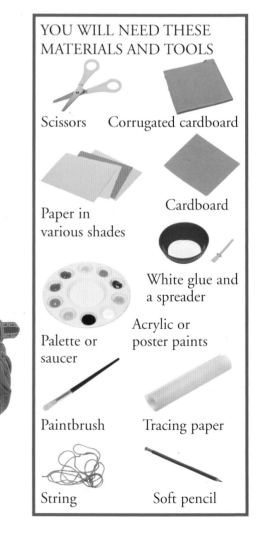

YOU WILL NEED THESE MATERIALS AND TOOLS

Scissors   Corrugated cardboard

Paper in various shades

Cardboard

White glue and a spreader

Palette or saucer

Acrylic or poster paints

Paintbrush   Tracing paper

String   Soft pencil

1 Cut a 12 x 16cm/5 x 6½in piece of cardboard. Cut small triangles from the spare cardboard and rectangles from the corrugated cardboard. Glue these around the edges of the piece.

2 When the glue is completely dry, paint the shapes on the cardboard. Use lots of different shades. Be careful not to get the shapes too wet, otherwise they might smudge.

3 Cut out pieces of paper the same size as the piece of cardboard. Line up the edges and corners of the cardboard and paper, and press down hard. Repeat for each sheet of paper.

4 While the papers are drying, make some envelopes. Using a soft pencil, trace the envelope template from the beginning of the book, then retrace it on to paper. Cut it out.

5 Follow the instructions on the envelope template to fold it and glue it together. Make one envelope for each sheet of paper.

6 Cut out a piece of cardboard the same size as the envelopes. Glue the string around the edge and paint it to make an interesting pattern.

7 Print the envelopes in the same way as you printed the paper.

Family and friends will soon know who is writing to them!

35

Finger-painted Flowers

These wild and pretty flowers will brighten up any room and don't even need to be watered! The great thing about making your own flowers is that you can choose which shades you want them to be and if you paint the backs and fronts differently, you can turn them around when you get bored.

Flower arranging
To make a beautiful flower arrangement put a piece of florist's foam or crumpled newspaper in the bottom of the vase. This will help to keep the flowers upright.

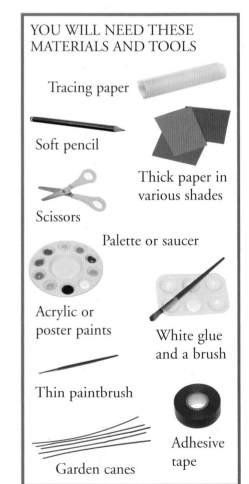

YOU WILL NEED THESE MATERIALS AND TOOLS

Tracing paper

Soft pencil

Thick paper in various shades

Scissors

Palette or saucer

Acrylic or poster paints

White glue and a brush

Thin paintbrush

Garden canes

Adhesive tape

36

1 Using a soft pencil, trace the flower, circle and leaf templates from the beginning of the book on to paper.

2 Using the scissors, cut out the shapes. You will need two matching flower shapes, two circles and two leaf shapes for each flower.

3 Glue a circle of paper on to the middle of each flower. Make sure that the flowers and the circles are different shades.

4 Dip your fingers one at a time into the paint and then press them on to your flowers. Use a different finger for each shade. Cover the flowers with finger prints.

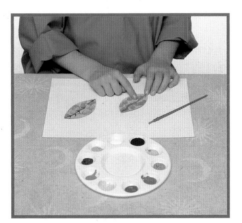

5 Leave the flowers to dry thoroughly while you make the leaves. Finger paint the leaf shapes with different green paints and paint a fine line of paint down the middle of each one to make the vein. Leave them to dry.

6 Use a piece of adhesive tape to attach a garden cane to the back of a flower. Glue a matching flower on to the back and gently press it down to make sure that it sticks.

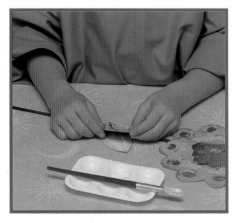

7 Attach the back of one leaf to the garden cane with adhesive tape and glue a matching leaf to the back of it.

Everlasting flowers brighten up even the dullest day.

Wooden Spoon Puppets

Tania and Joshua are having fun painting their puppets. Create your own play characters on wooden spoons then put on a show to impress the grown-ups. Hide behind the sofa and use its back as the stage. Try to give all the characters different voices, too.

Drying tip

Stand the spoons in a jar while the wet heads dry. To dry the handles, stand the heads in a big lump of non-hardening clay.

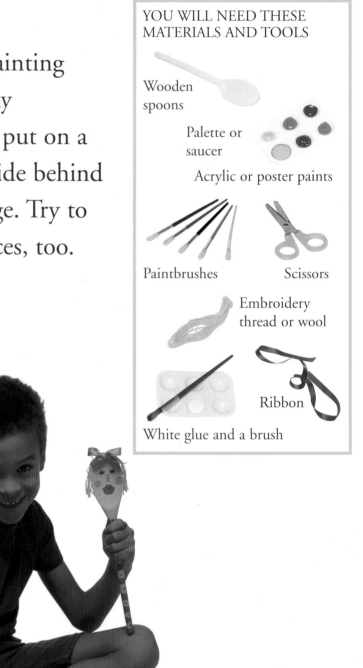

YOU WILL NEED THESE MATERIALS AND TOOLS

Wooden spoons

Palette or saucer

Acrylic or poster paints

Paintbrushes

Scissors

Embroidery thread or wool

Ribbon

White glue and a brush

1 Paint the head of the spoon and leave it to dry.

2 Paint the handle of the spoon using a different shade and leave it to dry.

3 Decorate the handle with spots, stripes, collar, buttons or a bow tie.

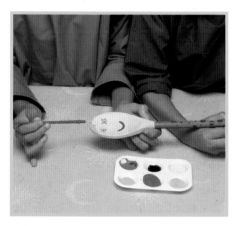

4 Paint a face on to the head of the spoon and leave to dry. Paint on some hair. If you are making a man puppet, you may choose to leave him with a bald head!

5 If you want to add long hair, cut about 15 strands of embroidery thread all the same length. Tie a shorter piece around the middle of them to keep them together.

6 Glue the hair on to the top of the puppet's head and leave it to dry. Try not to use too much glue. If you do, let it dry, then peel off the excess with your fingers.

Make your own mini-stage and impress your friends with your plays!

7 Tie the ribbon into a bow and glue it on to the hair.

39

The Projects

Wax-resist Badges

Add a personal touch to your outfit with a badge made with the magical technique of wax resist. Alice is using wax crayons, which give a bright result, but the technique also works in black and white if you use a candle to draw your design. Remember that as your badge is made out of cardboard, you can't wear it outside in the rain.

Age badges
A variation on this idea is to make an age badge for you or a friend, or your little brother or sister. Vary the shades to suit the personality of the wearer.

YOU WILL NEED THESE
MATERIALS AND TOOLS

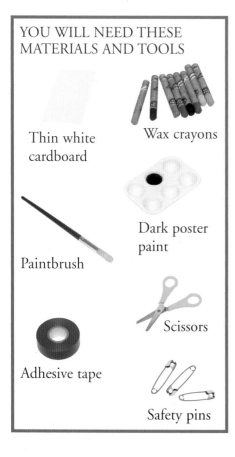

Thin white cardboard

Wax crayons

Dark poster paint

Paintbrush

Adhesive tape

Scissors

Safety pins

40

1 Collect together all the materials you will need for the project before you begin.

2 Draw a flowerpot shape on to the cardboard using wax crayons. The brighter the crayons, the more attractive the finished badge will be.

3 Draw on a cactus in a different shade, then decorate the pot and cactus using as many shades as you like.

4 Paint over your wax drawing with poster paint. Don't worry about the edges too much as you are going to cut out the picture later.

5 When the paint is completely dry, you should still be able to see your wax drawing. Cut around the edge of the cactus and flowerpot.

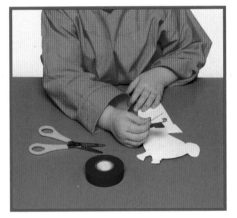

6 Turn the badge over. Cut a small piece of adhesive tape and use it to attach the safety pin to the middle of the badge.

It's obvious who's on your team with these bright badges!

Flowery Glass

These jolly flowers will liven up any glass frame. You could also use lots of smaller flower stickers to decorate a clear jar to use as a pencil pot or flower vase.

Aaron is decorating a picture frame, but you could stick the flowers on the inside of a real window if you like.

Handy hints
Plastic film is quite difficult to smooth down without getting air bubbles trapped. The trick is to work slowly, peeling off a bit of backing and smoothing as you go.

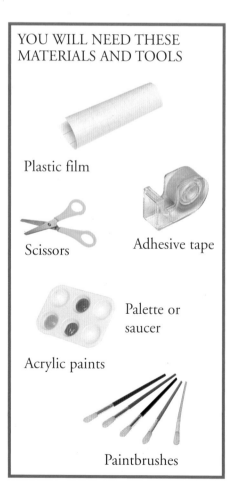

YOU WILL NEED THESE
MATERIALS AND TOOLS

Plastic film

Scissors

Adhesive tape

Palette or
saucer

Acrylic paints

Paintbrushes

1 Cut two pieces of plastic film the same size. Stick the corners of one piece to your work surface with tape. Do not remove the backing.

2 Paint the middle of a flower on to the middle of one piece of the film. Use a bright shade such as red, purple or yellow.

3 Using a different shade, paint five petals around the middle of the flower. Take care not to smudge the middle as you paint.

4 Decorate the flower with spots of a different, bright shade. Leave the flower to dry completely.

5 Take the second piece of film and carefully peel away the film's backing. Stick it over the flower. Work slowly, smoothing out any air bubbles with your fingers as you go.

6 If you get an air bubble, prick it with the point of a needle and smooth it out, then carefully cut around the flower.

7 Peel off the backing and stick the flower to the inside of your frame or window.

Enjoy year-round blooms on your flowery glass.

Flick-painted Scarscape

This is a messy project, so be sure to cover your work surface with lots of newspaper or scrap paper, or, if the weather is fine, do your flick painting outside. You can use any size of box for the planet story. The planet and rocket will move if you blow them or put the box by an open window.

If you want to make the inside of the box sparkle, add some glitter or cut out star shapes from kitchen foil and arrange them around the box.

Large-scale scene

A shoebox was used for this project but if you want to make a really big scene, get a box from the supermarket that had apples or oranges in it. Remember to make more than one of each mobile if you are using a big box.

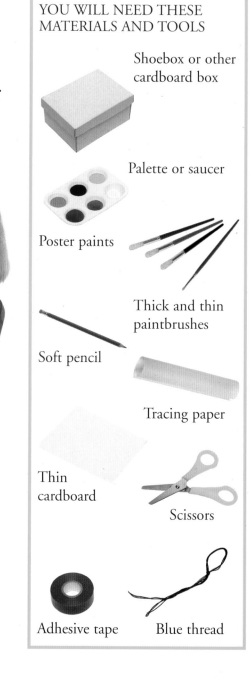

YOU WILL NEED THESE MATERIALS AND TOOLS

Shoebox or other cardboard box

Palette or saucer

Poster paints

Thick and thin paintbrushes

Soft pencil

Tracing paper

Thin cardboard

Scissors

Adhesive tape

Blue thread

1 Paint the shoebox inside and out using blue paint. You don't need the lid so don't bother with that. Leave the box to dry, then stand it on a wipe-clean surface, inside a cardboard box, or on a surface covered with newspaper.

2 Dip a medium-sized paintbrush in one of your pots of poster paint and flick the paint into the box. For fine splatters, tap the brush handle on the edge of the box. Repeat this with the different shades of paint.

3 Leave the box to dry thoroughly while you make the mobiles and decorations. Using a soft pencil, trace the star, planet and rocket templates from the beginning of the book on to pieces of cardboard.

4 Cut out the shapes. If your box is large, you will need more than one of each. You will also need some stars for the outside of the box.

5 Cover your work surface with scrap paper, then paint each shape. Choose yellow, gold or silver for the stars and bright shades for the planet and rocket.

6 Use a piece of adhesive tape to attach a length of blue thread to the shapes to hang inside the box. Glue some of the stars to the top and sides of the box.

7 Finally, tape the rocket and planet to the roof of the box.

Your space scene will amaze your friends.

ojects

Paint-combed Postcards

Receiving one of these jolly cards in the post will brighten up a special friend's day. You could also use the cards as party invitations, writing all the details – date, time and so on – on the back. Whatever you do with the cards, make sure that the paint is dry first.

Kirsty is making interesting patterns with a plastic picnic fork. You could, if you prefer, use a cookie cutter and twist it around in the paint to make a slightly different pattern. Remember to wash it well afterwards.

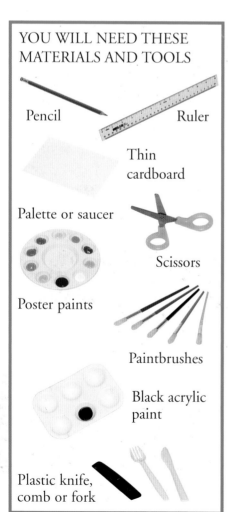

YOU WILL NEED THESE MATERIALS AND TOOLS

Pencil

Ruler

Thin cardboard

Palette or saucer

Scissors

Poster paints

Paintbrushes

Black acrylic paint

Plastic knife, comb or fork